from an LDS perspective

Agency and Accountability.
vital principles of the Gospel

THE BEST HELP IS
NO HELP

hard answers to hard questions
about helping
an addicted child or loved one

Table of Contents

Forward

Warning!

Introduction

Chapters   **Page**

1 - A Weighty Matter 1

2 - What Do You Know About Agency? 2

3 - Agency in the Garden of Eden 4

4 - Freedom Isn't Free 5

5 - So What? 7

6 - What Have We Learned So Far? 8

7 - Hard Questions 10

8 - And Hard Answers 14

9 - No Respecter of Persons 15

10 - Boundaries = Rules = Commandments 16

11 - Not Curable - Definitely Controllable (but not by us) 17

12 - We're in This Together 18

13 - The Learning Curve 19

14 - The Dilemma 20

15 - How is That? 21

16 - Just This One More Time! 22

17 - Facts From Fiction 23

18 - In a Nut Shell 24

19 - Onward 26

Acknowledgments

FORWARD

After you have raised your child, doing the very best you can, after that child has begun to exercise their agency, what they decide is in their hands. It is their agency, their life.

If the decisions they make are not in keeping with the standards of the Gospel, what do you, the parents, do? After you have reasoned with them, pled with them, cried over them and constantly prayed for them, what are you going to do?

After you have helped them out of numerous jams, laid down the law, given them one more chance (again), had them sign contracts, paid their debts, bailed them out of jail, pulled whatever strings you have, bought them a car or two, paid their rent, yet they continue in the path of self-destructive behavior, what do you do next?

We, and countless other parents have tried all of the above, and even more, with the same outcome.

What to do next?

What follows is what we and many others have found to be the best solution.

Is it guaranteed to work? No. Is it a full proof plan? No. But it is your best hope. It will seem to fly in the face of all you've been taught about being a parent and about love. It will be difficult, extremely so. But I believe it offers the best chance your loved one will have to be able, with the Lord's help, to defeat the demons which beset them.

I have no initials behind my name. My education comes from needing help and seeking that help.

From learning what works and what doesn't. Experience.

I don't claim to know it all, or even much. What I present comes from what I have learned as I moved from being the head of an "ideal" Mormon family to the reality of being the father of an alcoholic/addict. I have learned that the way you help someone with addictions is way different from our concepts of help.

The hard truths come from addicts in recovery. By their own admissions, addicts are liars, cheats, thieves, and manipulators. They are only concerned with

themselves and the moment! Addiction has skewed their entire thinking patterns. In order to help them we must accept these initially unacceptable facts, and learn a new way of thinking ourselves.

While our ultimate hope is to heal them, we must come to accept the fact that no matter how hard we try, we cannot do it. If it is to happen, they must do it themselves with the help of the Lord. Hopefully this book will help each of its readers do what they can do–find acceptance and understanding and strength–to be able to offer this seemingly un-Christ-like "help" to their suffering loved ones.

ii

WARNING!

You may think, as you read this material, that it seems redundant.

It is redundant!

You are about to read the same material repeatedly –

sometimes in a different sentence structure – and sometimes just repeatedly.

Why?

Because if we are going to get it

we, parents,

NEED to hear it

OVER AND OVER AND OVER!

INTRODUCTION

My name is Dave. Gail and I have been married 44 years. We are the parents of six and the grandparents of ten. Our youngest child is an addict/alcoholic. He has been "clean and sober" for a little more than a year and a half.

By now we are what we call "cautiously optimistic". I don't know how long the cautious part lasts, probably for years, because it takes years of hope and then disappointment to reach the state of hopelessness that the parents and alcoholics/addicts finally reach. Hopes raise, then are dashed by the behavior of your loved one time after time. Our son has given his permission, and his approval, to share this message.

I've been a member of the Church of Jesus Christ of Latter-day Saints for over 50 years. In that length of time it's been my responsibility to serve in several bishoprics and observe many people in a variety of situations. Consequently, I have been able to witness the behavior of probably hundreds of young people and see family dynamics in action. In addition, I was employed as a deputy sheriff for

Los Angeles County – both on the streets and in the jail.

Gail and I have served time at Purgatory Correctional Facility in Southern Utah. Let me reword that. Gail and I have served together at Purgatory, teaching religion classes. Incidentally, there are very few places more appropriately named than Purgatory Correctional Facility. While there we learned much about the behavior of the people who find themselves in jail, usually multiple times. Basically good people who made poor choices.

Essentially, what got them where they are is the same – the same behavior pattern.

This book has evolved over a period of time, beginning with endless soul-searching, with short written articles and a lengthier Sacrament meeting talk. It is the result of seeing the pain and suffering of so many other parents, all of us struggling with these same problems, the same feelings of helplessness and hopelessness, and the same confusions over how best to help.

The following is a sometimes painful message from the heart. I have neither taken the time to smooth out rough spots nor cover all topics. I feel getting the message out now is more important than attempting to polish it.

Chapter 1 - A Weighty Matter

I recently got on the scale and found that I weigh 200 lbs. According to the U.S. Department of Health I am more than 25 lbs. overweight. And it's Gail's fault. If she were not such a good cook I would not eat so much and consequently, I would not weigh so much.

Let's face it, I have a terrible habit, I overeat. Someone help me, please. Take away my extra pounds. Take away my terrible habit. But better yet, let me keep my terrible habit but take away the consequence.

However, as much as I would like to blame Gail or anyone else, I can't. It is my habit, so it is my consequences. Do I have to have a heart attack before I stop overeating? Maybe I will.

Who must solve this problem? Why can't you do it for me?

Until I take ownership/responsibility for my actions there will be no change in my behavior. As long as I try to push the responsibility off on someone else, I will do nothing about my problem. Or, as long as someone else takes responsibility for my actions I will do nothing about it.

I guarantee you, as long as we do not let those we love realize the consequences of their behavior, the behavior will not change. No matter how much we want them to change it will not happen until they are held accountable for their actions.

We cheat our children when we take away their agency/accountability – the consequences of their actions, whether they be little children or teenagers or adults.

We cheat the Lord's plan of agency when we do not let them experience the consequences of their action.

Even though we might think we are doing something good and noble for them, we are in fact doing them a terrible disservice. We are harming them, stunting their growth, both in this life and in eternity.

It is vital that we realize <u>and accept</u> the fact that

1

WE DIDN'T   CAUSE IT!

WE CAN'T   CONTROL IT!

WE CAN'T   CURE IT!

Chapter 2 - What do we know about agency?

What do we know about the history and the place of agency and accountability in the eternal plan?

We know that it existed in the pre-existent councils in heaven. Councils in which we were all participants. In fact we know that the "war in heaven" was fought over the agency of all of Heavenly Father's children.

From the *Pearl of Great Price* we learn much of agency and its inseparable twin, accountability.

In the book of Abraham the scene is set for the future and the pattern for all the spirits that existed.

Abraham 3: 24-28

    24 And there stood one among them that was like unto God, and he said unto those who were with him: We will go down, for there is space there, and we will take of these materials, and we will make an earth whereon these may dwell;

    25 And we will prove them herewith, to see if they will do all things whatsoever the Lord their God shall command them;

    26 And they who keep their first estate shall be added upon; and they who keep not their first estate shall not have glory in the same kingdom with those who keep their first estate; and they who keep their second estate shall have glory added upon their heads for ever and ever.

    27 And the Lord said: Whom shall I send? And one answered like unto the Son of Man: Here am I, send me. And another answered and said: Here am I, send me. And the Lord said: I will send the first.

    28 And the second was angry, and kept not his first estate; and, at that day, many followed after him.

Read the next scripture in inverse order. It will not change the meaning, only the stress.

Moses 4: 2

    2 But, behold, my Beloved Son, which was my Beloved and Chosen from the beginning, said unto me—Father, thy will be done, and the glory be thine forever.

Moses 4: 1

    1 And I, the Lord God, spake unto Moses, saying: That Satan, whom thou hast commanded in the name of mine Only Begotten, is the same which was from the beginning, and he came before me, saying—Behold, here am I, send me, I will be thy son, and I will redeem all mankind, that one soul shall not be lost, and surely I will do it; wherefore give me thine honor.

Christ will do the will of the Father. Satan volunteers to come and "redeem all mankind, that not one soul shall be lost." I think it is interesting that Satan uses the word redeem. And that everyone would be redeemed. Redeemed from what?

Moses 4: 3

    3 Wherefore, because that Satan rebelled against me, and sought to destroy the agency of man, which I, the Lord God, had given him, and also, that I should give unto him mine own power; by the power of mine Only Begotten, I caused that he should be cast down;

Satan sought to destroy the agency of man. In my opinion I do not think Satan cared what we would do, whether we kept the commandments or not, if his plan would have been accepted. I don't think he cared if we sinned or didn't sin, he was going to haul us back to our Heavenly Father and there would have been no accountability. He would have "redeemed" us with no accountability or consequences to us. But whatever the case, the War in Heaven was fought and Satan and his followers were cast out over the issue of Agency/accountability.

Chapter 3 - Agency in the Garden of Eden

Moses 3:15-17   Thou shalt surely die. Verse 17 gives us the pattern of agency. Commandment, Agency/choice and Accountability/consequence.

Moses 3: 15-17
>   *15 And I, the Lord God, took the man, and put him into the Garden of Eden, to dress it, and to keep it.*
>   *16 And I, the Lord God, commanded the man, saying: Of every tree of the garden thou mayest freely eat,*
>   *17 But of the tree of the knowledge of good and evil, thou shalt not eat of it, nevertheless, thou mayest choose for thyself, for it is given unto thee; but, remember that I forbid it, for in the day thou eatest thereof thou shalt surely die.*

Enter Satan, he that was cast out with his followers, those who exercised their agency one last time when they chose to follow Satan. Who chose to surrender their agency. Satan "... the Father of all lies..." comes to Eve to tempt her.

From the Bible in Gen. 3:1-4, Satan tells Eve   ... *Thou shalt not surely die...*

Moses 4:10
>10 And the serpent said unto the woman: Ye shall not surely die;

What was the lie that Satan told to Eve? That was the simple lie he told. What is the bigger lie? That there would be no accountability for her actions. **The lie was, there would be no accountability!**

Moses 4:19   Later the Lord asked Eve to account for her action. She said, "The serpent beguiled me...." Or in other words, cheated or deceived her.
>*19 And I, the Lord God, said unto the woman: What is this thing which thou hast done? And the woman said: The serpent beguiled me, and I did eat.*

4
Chapter 4 - Freedom Isn't Free

Lehi, prior to his death takes the opportunity to teach his children one last time. Among other things he teaches of the atonement and redemption and the necessity of opposition in the Eternal plan. Included in that opposition is punishment. All men are to be judged in this plan or the plan is null and void. In fact opposition is a sign of the plan, for without it there is nothing.

We read in *The Book of Mormon:*

2 Nephi 2:10-13
>*10 And because of the intercession for all, all men come unto God; wherefore, they stand in the presence of him, to be judged of him according to the truth and holiness which is in him. Wherefore, the ends of the law which the Holy One hath given, unto the inflicting of the punishment which is affixed, which punishment that is affixed is in opposition to that of the happiness which is affixed, to answer the ends of the atonement—*
>
>*11 For it must needs be, that there is an opposition in all things. If not so, my first-born in the wilderness, righteousness could not be brought to pass, neither wickedness, neither holiness nor misery, neither good nor bad. Wherefore, all things must needs be a compound in one; wherefore, if it should be one body it must needs remain as dead, having no life neither death, nor corruption nor incorruption, happiness nor misery, neither sense nor insensibility.*
>
>*12 Wherefore, it must needs have been created for a thing of naught;*

wherefore there would have been no purpose in the end of its creation. Wherefore, this thing must needs destroy the wisdom of God and his eternal purposes, and also the power, and the mercy, and the justice of God.
   13 And if ye shall say there is no law, ye shall also say there is no sin. If ye shall say there is no sin, ye shall also say there is no righteousness. And if there be no righteousness there be no happiness. And if there be no righteousness nor happiness there be no punishment nor misery. And if these things are not there is no God. And if there is no God we are not, neither the earth; for there could have been no creation of things, neither to act nor to be acted upon; wherefore, all things must have vanished away.

Lehi goes on to tell us that man "... knowing good from evil..." are to act for themselves, and by their actions they choose "liberty and Eternal Life" by obedience to the Law, or they choose captivity and death by disobeying the

5

commandments. In other words, they experience the consequences of their actions,. We call the process, agency and accountability.

2 Ne. 2: 25-27
   25 Adam fell that men might be; and men care, that they might have joy.
   26 And the Messiah cometh in the fulness of time, that he may redeem the children of men from the fall. And because that they are redeemed from the fall they have become free
      forever, knowing good from evil; to act for themselves and not to be acted upon, save it be by the punishment of the law at the great and last day, according to the commandments which God hath given.

   27 Wherefore, men are free according to the flesh; and call things are given them which are expedient unto man. And they are free to choose liberty and eternal life, through the great Mediator of all men, or to choose captivity and death, according to the captivity and power of the devil; for he seeketh that all men might be miserable like unto himself.

Nephi quotes at length from Isaiah, after which he teaches of some of the false doctrine which will be promulgated in the latter days. Among them we find,

2 Nephi 28:7 *Eat drink and be merry....* The accountability has been removed.

Also in 2 Ne. 2: 28
      28 And now, my sons, I would that ye should look to the great Mediator, and hearken unto his great commandments; and be faithful unto his words, and choose eternal life, according to the will of his Holy Spirit;

Now from the *Doctrine and Covenants* we can read what the Lord has taught us about agency/accountability.

D&C 101: 78

78 That every man may act in doctrine and principle pertaining to futurity, according to the moral agency which I have given unto him, that every man may be accountable for his own sins in the day of judgment.

Elder Bruce R. McConkie, in *Mormon Doctrine*, page 15, "Personal accountability for all of one's acts underlies the whole gospel plan and is the natural outgrowth of the law of free agency. Without such personal responsibility free agency could not operate, for neither rewards nor punishments would follow the exercise of agency. And if there were no rewards or punishment, there would be no salvation or damnation, and so the whole plan of salvation would vanish away.(2 Nephi 2:11-16)"

Chapter 5 - So What?

So what does all of that have to do with us, today? Let's see if we can make it apply in our lives.

It is not my desire to offend anyone by what I am about to say, but undoubtedly I will. Much of this will hurt initially but many of us need to hear these words. Some of you may be tempted to think "These things don't really apply to me" or "My case is exceptional." Think again. And think carefully before you say that.

What I hope happens is some of you will consider the things I have to say and perhaps recognize some changes which need to be made.

I want to reiterate at this point, I have been through some of the same situations I'm addressing. We have faced the same decisions and the same uncertainties and the same conflicted feelings I'll talk about. They are part of being a parent, and a part of being one of our Heavenly Father's children.

President Wilford Woodruff said: "This agency has always been the heritage of man under the rule and government of God. He possessed it in the heaven of heavens before the world was, and the Lord maintained and defended it there against the aggression of Lucifer and those that took sides with him... .By virtue of this agency you and I and all mankind are made responsible beings, responsible for the course we pursue, the lives we live and the deeds we do."

By extension I will add that our children, having reached the age of accountability, are "responsible beings', responsible for the course **they** pursue, the lives **they** live and the deeds **they** do.

Chapter 6 - What have we learned so far?

Okay, what have we learned about agency?

We have learned that it is the Lord's eternal plan. And we have learned that accountability is an integral part of that plan. There cannot exist choices without consequences. To try to separate them was Satan's plan, not God's plan.

So what is our responsibility in the agency/accountability aspect of the Lord's plan? I see it as twofold..

1. First and obviously, we must make this concept live in our own lives.

2. Teaching our children accountability.

There are four words which may be interchangeable in this discussion; I'll use each of them.
accountability (obviously)
consequences
results
responsibility

We must teach our children from a young age that they must be responsible for their actions. From the breaking of family rules to the breaking of family standards to the breaking of laws to the breaking of the commandments.

We must begin to teach them at an early age. In fact the teaching should begin as soon as they are able to understand. Thus it becomes a part of them. I realize that our expectation of a two year old is not the same as a six year old or a twelve year old, but each is capable of learning at their own level of understanding.

I assure you, the longer we wait to teach them the more difficult will be the task. We should not wait until they are eight years old or teenagers, or in way too many cases until they are well into adulthood to teach them. If we do so we have given ourselves, and our children an onerous task.

How will our children learn accountability if we do not teach them and if we do not hold them accountable for the things which they do or fail to do? In fact the Lord has given us that responsibility.

D&C 68: 25-26
25 And again, inasmuch as parents have children in Zion, or in any of her stakes which are organized, that teach them not to understand the doctrine of

repentance, faith in Christ the Son of the living God, and of baptism and the gift of the Holy Ghost by the laying on of the hands, when eight years old, the sin be upon the heads of the parents.

26 For this shall be a law unto the inhabitants of Zion, or in any of her stakes which are organized.

D&C 93: 40
40 But I have commanded you to bring up your children in light and truth.

How do we teach our children this concept? We teach them by setting boundaries, establishing rules, having expectations, and making our children adhere to those rules, etc. When they fail to comply with rules, etc, there must be consequences. We are not doing our children any favors when we fail to hold them responsible for their actions, or in many cases, inaction.

We must teach our families the accountability of agency and we must let them experience that, or we are cheating them.

In fact, whose plan are we following when we remove or try to remove our loved one's accountability? Or try to avoid it for ourselves by making someone else responsible for our actions?

To try to avoid accountability or to try and remove accountability for someone else is contrary to the Lord's plan.

You know we cannot redeem or remove from our loved ones the consequences of their action. That is not within our power.

If we don't teach them and let them be accountable, all we are doing is postponing the inevitable. For they are learning habits and traits which they will some day have to pay for. Because ultimately, they cannot avoid the consequences for their actions.

Chapter 7 - Hard Questions

It may seem to you that it is a hard thing to teach your young children to be accountable for their actions, but I assure you, it is a much harder thing to try to teach them as teenagers or adults.

We do our family members a terrible disservice when we do not hold them accountable for their own behavior. Or when things don't go the way they would like and we try to make things better. In fact we are taking from our loved one the opportunity to grow from their adversity.

President James Faust said "In giving time to his children, a father should be able to demonstrate that he has enough love for them to command them as well as discipline them. Children want and need discipline. As they approach some dangers, they are silently pleading, 'Don't let me do it.' President David O. McKay has said that, 'If we do not adequately discipline our children, society will discipline them in a way we may not like.' Wise discipline reinforces the dimensions of eternal love. This reinforcement will bring great security into their lives."   *Ensign,* First Presidency Message, September, 2006

Perhaps we should ask ourselves a few questions when we consider withholding accountability.

Why am I doing this?

Am I doing it for my loved one or am I doing it for me?

Am I doing it because it is the easy way out, rather than confronting them with their behavior and its consequences?

What good am I doing for them?

What harm am I ultimately doing to them?

What should I be doing in this situation?

Whose fault is it that they are in this situation?

Who is responsible for getting them out of it?

What harm is it doing to **you** to be in this situation?

What is it doing to or for your relationship with them?

What are we teaching them about agency when we try to ease or remove their accountability?

And ask yourself this question, "Who is going to help them when you are no longer able to, and they haven't learned to do it for themselves?" When will they learn to grow? If we enable them now, when will they learn to be accountable for their choices? When will it be too late for them to learn?

The very best help you can give them is to let them be responsible for their actions, let **them** be accountable.

We must let our children learn to be accountable by letting them be accountable.

We stifle them, we inhibit their growth when we try to ease them through the tough times they have created for themselves.

We cripple them by trying to or by removing the results of their actions.

Ordinarily positive change will not occur until parents allow their children to experience the consequences of bad decisions.

The following is an excerpt from an article in the *Ensign,* July 2006, Pg 61. The name was changed.

"Lance, a young adult living at home, was doing just about everything wrong. He lied, stole, cheated, and used drugs and alcohol. He was unchaste and seemed completely indifferent to how his actions affected his parents and other family members. His mother and father had tried everything they could think of to help him. For several years they had been patient and forgiving. They convinced him to see a professional counselor, but after a session or two he refused to go back. He never did agree to see his bishop. Finally, Lance was arrested.

The phone rang at Lance's home, and his mother answered. "Hi, Mom, this is Lance. I'm in jail, and they won't let me out until you come and get me. Please hurry!"

Lance's mother was shocked, even panicked, but didn't say anything. Lance pleaded again, "Mom, please hurry! This is not a nice place!"

She didn't say anything for a long time, then quietly asked, "Lance, are you guilty of the charges?"

"Well, Mom, I really wasn't as involved as the police say I was."

"Lance, are you guilty?"

"Well, Mom, I guess I am."

Then, with all the courage she could muster, she replied, "I'm sorry that you are. I guess you will have to work through this by yourself. Call me when you get it all worked out." She hung up the phone and fell apart.

Two very long days passed. Finally, Lance called, and his parents went to the police station to pick him up. A few more days passed, and the phone rang again. Lance's mother answered, and this time it was an attorney.

"Hello. I am Mark Johnson. I helped Lance with his legal problems while he was in custody. I just wanted to speak with you to see how you wanted to work out my compensation for helping Lance get out of jail."

At first Lance's mother was troubled. Finances were tight, and she was surprised at the call. She paused a minute, then said, "Mr. Johnson, I appreciate what you did to help Lance, but you are talking to the wrong person. I did not hire you. You did not help me. You helped Lance. If you want compensation for your efforts, I think you ought to talk to Lance."

Some time later, Lance came to his parents asking for a "donation" to pay his legal bill, but the donation did not come. Lance had to go back to the attorney and work out a pay-back plan. After many months of payments, Lance paid Mr. Johnson in full. Lance eventually returned to activity in the Church and is doing very well as a student at a major university. He is paying for much of his education himself, and his relationship with his parents couldn't be better. He will tell you today that the actions of his very brave and very frightened mother helped him turn his life around.

Obviously, not all stories have such a happy ending. However, many stories do, if parents wait long enough and if they are willing to do the right thing.

Parents are accountable to teach their children to take responsibility for their actions. This is almost always a very hard thing to do and often may involve what seems to be a temporary abandonment. In a very real sense, parents can interfere with their children's progress if they try to protect them from the consequences of their actions.

Our prototype here is Heavenly Father and His response to Adam and Eve after they had partaken of the forbidden fruit. He cast them out of the Garden of Eden, and to help them learn, He cursed the ground for their sake (see Gen. 3:17). While He promises that His grace will be sufficient for us, grace will not replace our experiencing consequences that are necessary to teach us something we need to know."

    Again, Who are we helping when we enable, remove the accountability, of our loved ones?
    How is it a help?
    How are we harming them?
    Or, are we really doing it for ourselves?
    What is the good we may do by constantly helping?
    What is the harm?

Actions and inactions really do effect others. When there is an addict or an alcoholic in your family you definitely know there is an effect. When there is a law breaker in the family you know you are effected. When a child, teenager or adult in the home chooses to be disobedient you know there is an effect on those around. But if there is not an immediate, personal effect, is there no accountability?

Another problem with having an addicted love one in the home is the damaging creation of a "wedge." Whether done purposely or in advertently by the addict, their behavior often causes parents to become at odds on the best way to help their child. One may want to offer as much help as possible while the other may want to take a "hard line." Contention often is the outcome, driving the couple apart.

Our society has become a society of debt and bankruptcy. Why? Because we indulge ourselves, then we feel no obligation to pay. Why? Because we have learned that someone else will take care of it for us. They always have. Because we have learned that we finally won't be held accountable for our debts. (Incidently, Utah is at the top of the list for bankruptcy filings per capita. That is an appalling statistic.)

Chapter 8 - And Hard Answers

It needs to be understood that I am not saying you shouldn't be helping you children and one another in their legitimate needs. Obviously not. That is always appropriate. I am talking about enabling in harmful, habitual decisions? When they are misbehaving they need to be to be disciplined. They need to be held responsible for their actions/behavior.

The value of the word NO! What is wrong with NO? We, our society, went through a time when parents didn't want to say the "N" word to their children. I never did figure that one out. I wonder if we are experiencing the fallout from that misguided time period. We indulge ourselves and then indulge our children. And then we or they don't know how to face the results of the decisions that were made.

The value of consequences. Until they come to understand that there really are consequences for actions they will continue to choose to do wrong or make wrong decisions.

Last year, in Sunday School we learned about agency and accountability. Good choices, good results: bad choices, bad results. In fact, when the Children of Israel proved to the Lord that they were going to continue to make stupid decisions he was done with them. They were on their own to face the consequences. I think there is a parallel here. I think we would be terribly remiss to "carry" our children once they have shown they won't get it together until we make them get it together.

We are not our children's friend, we are their parent. The friendship part comes later.

Sometimes, even when it is not their fault they need to fix it, work it out for themselves. To get through the adversity, to grow from the experience. We deprive them when we fix it for them.

Adversity is a necessity.   We must not try to take that away from our family.

No one will learn if we don't let them? What lesson are we teaching when we take away our loved one's accountability?

We do not have the power to redeem our children from their poor choices.

We do a terrible disservice to our children, both young and old, when we take from them their accountability, the consequences of their actions.

When we remove any part of agency, including accountability we are endorsing Satan's plan of taking from us our agency.

Chapter 9 - No Respecter of Persons

Paramount in our lives are our children. We know that the most important responsibility we can have is to raise our children in the way of the Lord. We are living in a society that makes no demands and expects no accountability. Do not let that extend into your families.

We must teach agency and accountability. Then, though it may seem contrary to our responsibility, after we have taught them we must let them apply those teachings in their lives. If we have done our job in teaching them as we've raised them, then we have done our job. Now it is up to them to use that agency they have been given by our Heavenly Father, and then be accountable for their actions.

Addiction, no matter what kind of addiction, is no respecter of persons, nor respecter of positions in a family.

If it's the oldest child, we say "We were too hard on him." If it is the youngest child we say "We were too easy on him." If it was the middle child, we'd say "It was because he is the----in the middle!"

Just as the words addict and alcoholic are used interchangeably, when we are speaking about children the word is also interchangeable, to include spouses, parents or siblings or other adults with abuse and accountability problems.

Position in the family is never the issue. Agency always is.

Chapter 10 - Boundaries = Rules = Commandments

Is there no other way to learn about choices/agency and accountability?

Our son had been addicted for many years before we realized it. Next, we had to admit it. Over time things didn't improve. Troubles increased.

For several months the three of us went to a psychologist to try to learn how we could all cope and work through this situation. We learned a lot, but no significant change took place in his behavior. After six months of weekly visits the therapist told our son that everyone was working hard at his recovery, except for our son. Things continued down hill.

Finally he was arrested---again. This time he applied to Drug Court, a tough but fantastic opportunity available here in Southern Utah.

This step was probably the most important decision he could have made. It was his admission that he needed help. Drug Court gives him tools to learn to be accountable, and gives him the incentive to stay the course, because if he fails to do so there are unavoidable results.

His agency is not removed. Each day he must make the choice if he is going to continue to choose well and make the wise decisions. And if he chooses not to, the consequence is fixed. Similar to the Lord's plan of agency.

Chapter 11 - While Not Curable - Definitely Controllable (but not by us)

His acceptance into Drug Court has provided us with the opportunity to learn more of what our son is going through, to come to grips with the facts that
1) addiction is a hideous disease, very often with genetic predisposition.

    2) that, while it is not curable, it is controllable. Just like many other diseases or illnesses.

    3) it is extremely hard to control, even when the intentions are the very best.   Addicts cannot overcome it on their own. God, the higher power, is there   to help them when they are ready for that help,

    4) but it will not happen one minute before they are ready, no matter how hard <u>we</u> try nor how badly <u>we</u> want it.

He attends a number of and variety of meetings weekly, including group sessions, private sessions, reporting to the judge, LDS 12 -step programs, and a variety of Alcoholics Anonymous meetings, as well as those geared to various other addictions. There are many rules and responsibilities. They are required to become accountable in all aspects of their daily lives. Recovery is a life-style change. Recovery is a full-time, life-time effort. And recovery is not limited to the "recoverer."

It is important to note here, The Addict must be ready to begin recovery and the one that must do the work. No matter how much we want to help, we can not do it for them. We want to make it easier, but we must not. We must memorize the following truth.

We didn't cause it.

We can't control it.

We can't cure it.

Chapter 12 - We're in This Together

It is common for those suffering from alcohol and other addictions to claim that they are hurting no one but themselves. Wrong! Everyone suffers! Gail and I attend a support group made up of the family members of addicts and alcoholics, most of which are clients of Drug Court. In this group we learn coping skills and the correct actions and reactions to the many situations we face. Al-Anon and Al-a-Teen are similar groups, also offering help and support for family members of addicts.

Almost universally, the reaction after attending the first meeting or two is, "No, this is not for me." "My situation is different." "These are not my kind of people." If they keep coming, it doesn't take very long to see all that is offered— support, understanding, education, strength, help and love. Again, addiction is no respecter of persons, and we really are those kind of people.

Just as addicts cannot heal themselves on their own; these various groups are available to help family members heal themselves.

Chapter 13 - The Learning Curve

The most often heard laments we hear from newcomers at the family group we attend go like this, "It's my baby." "It's my child." "I have to help them."

And the most common way the parent chooses to help is--- to remove some or all of the consequences from their child. This is not helping! Again, removing consequences, "rescuing" our loved ones from the consequences of their actions, is not helping them! It is ENABLING them!

Until our children learn that they must be accountable for their own actions, that someone else is not going to pick up the pieces for them, they will continue to make poor choices. (Poor is a euphemism for dumb or stupid.)

Another often heard explanation for bailing their child out of a jam is this. "If I help them just this one more time, if I get them out of just one more jam, they'll learn their lesson and their life will turn around."

We truly want to believe that, but overwhelming statistics tell us that is not going to happen. Until they have to pay the price for their own actions they'll continue in their way--an almost 100% guarantee.

A recovering addict, who is also part of our family group in support of his fiancee' said, "I would not face my own problems as long as there was someone else to take care of them for me. It was not until I ran out of options, not until I was literally sleeping in the alley and diving in the dumpster for food, that I became responsible to find my own solution."

The mother of this same young man finally (after many years of bailing him out) told him, "I'm sorry I never let you have the privilege of failing."

Think of the significance of that statement. It is profound. "I'm sorry I <u>never let you</u> have the <u>privilege of failing</u>."

These important principles apply not just to the addicted, but to all those who, through their own poor decisions have put themselves in a jam.

This does not mean that we can't help our kids when they need our help on occasion. We are referring to those who seem to habitually get them selves in a spot and we, the parents keep bailing them out. For them the cord needs to be cut, for their good as well as ours.

Chapter 14 - The Dilemma

We, as members of the Church seem to have a dilemma. It is strongly stressed over and over that our family is the greatest responsibility we will ever have. And, that we are to love unconditionally. Both are true. So how do these equate to letting our child go to jail? Or letting them pay their own debts, or letting them go homeless. (Try dropping off your child at a homeless shelter some day. We did.)

This is the time we must again ask the hard questions

What is, in the long run (In the eternal scheme), the very best thing for
    my child?
Is it better to bail them out of jail or let them do their time?
Is it better to pay their debt or let them be responsible for it?
    Is it better to pay their rent or buy them food because they chose to spend their money on drugs or alcohol, or just overspend on frivolous stuff, or lost their job because of irresponsibility, or because they are in no condition to hold down a job---or let them find their own way out of their own problem?

Which of these choices would best teach them? What do we tend to do? How often do we start trying to solve their problem for them?

The hard answer to the hard questions is one of compassion and concern. It is the answer of unconditional love: When our loved one comes to us with a situation they have gotten themself into we need to respond, "That is a problem, what are you going to do about it?"

It's not the easy thing to do but it is the right thing to do, the necessary thing to do. Trust me when I say that my tongue has been very sore, from bitting it so hard to keep from stepping in–or stepping up.

Before you say, "But my case is special. We are not like that. My child is going to turn their life around when I help them this one more time," let me say, Don't bet the farm on it!

So where is the parent in this? Where is the Christianity in this?

Again, the question we need to ask is, "What is <u>the best thing</u> I can do for my son or daughter? Again ask, "What is the best thing for me as well?"

Chapter 15 - How Is That?

We were shocked to learn that when we help someone do something they should be doing for themselves there is resentment. What's the shock? Of course, we resent it! No, the shock is ---- There is also resentment on the part of the receiver, not that they would ever admit it, and will take whatever they can get.

You give, they take, sometimes they demand and you give.

From our perspective it doesn't make sense that there is also real resentment at this time, on their part. But we have learned that there is little about the workings of an addicted brain that makes sense.

They take---and they resent you for giving---for the implication that they can't do it themselves.

Isn't that what we are saying when we take on their accountability, that the individual can't do it on their own?

Does it mean they can't make it on their own,
or
we think they can't make it on their own,
or
they perceive we think they can't make it on their own.

Resentment on both sides.

That is how!

Chapter 16 - Just This One More Time!

(And again, you know that we are not talking about the responsible family member who may have an occasional emergency arise.)

There is the very real tendency for us to say, at least to ourselves, "If I help them just this one time, or one more time, this will be what they need to get them over the hump, started in the right direction."

In our family group meeting we were shown a segment of an episode of "The Simpsons."

Bart, as usual, has caused problems, and has been sent to bed without super. He isn't worried. Time passes and he is getting hungry. More time passes and all the lights go out. Now he is worried. His parents have always relented before. He is hungry.

And he is very worried, realizing that the time appears to have finally come that he is going to have to shape up.

The very next instant, his door opens and his dad sneaks in with a plate of pizza and an admonition of love and "I know you will try to do better...."

Bart thanks his dad profusely and, after the door closes adds----
"Sucker."

Chapter 17 - Facts From Fiction

The fact is: Until they are <u>made to do it for themselves</u> <u>they will not do it</u> <u>for themselves.!</u>

The fact is: We deprive our loved ones of gaining the full benefits of agency when we remove their accountability.

The fact is: We are living in a society that makes no demands and expects no accountability. Enabling generates a feeling of entitlement which evolves into expectations and demands.

If we do not enable them, if we do not remove their accountability, does it mean we love them any less? NO! the opposite is true.

We don't help them because we DO love them!

They won't see this at the time, but at some future time they will understand.

Young adult children and teenagers are responsible for their decisions and the consequences. It is difficult for us, the parents or in some cases the spouse, to let the consequences take effect. We want to step up and make it easier on our child or spouse, hoping that they have learned their lesson and are ready to turn their life around. Overwhelming statistics tell us that this isn't going to happen. Until they are held accountable for their decisions they will continue on the same path.

Those of us in the Church, who have been taught that our families are our most important responsibility, feel we are abdicating that responsibility when we seemingly turn our back on our child in need.

I suggest we are performing a greater disservice when we take away their agency by removing the consequence for their actions.

Also, as parents, we have a tendency to blame ourselves for the actions of our children. Wrong! If we have done our job as a parent, if we have taught our kids right from wrong, if we have done our best to teach them the right way-- then we have done our job. Our children have, and must be permitted to use their agency. We essentially are taking on Satan's plan when we remove any part of the agency process.

Chapter 18 - In a Nut Shell

I hope that I have been able to help you see that we are each accountable for our actions and our loved one must be accountable for their's.

And that:

1. Our job is not to be our children's friends, we are their parents. The friendship part comes later, as they grow and mature.

2. Boundaries, rules, responsibility, obedience and commandments are not bad words, and they need to be enforced and reinforced on a regular basis. And not only for problem kids. This is the way our children, from a very young age begin to learn to make decisions.

They need to learn to make good decisions. They need to learn to be responsible. And they need to continue to be taught about choices and the results of those choices–agency and accountability. This is the best way to help keep them from becoming "problem kids."

3. We are doing our loved one, young and old, a terrible disservice when we take from them their accountability---the consequences of their actions.

What lesson are we teaching our children if we do not let them be accountable for the things they do, the choices they ---- chose?

4. When we remove any part of agency, including accountability we are endorsing Satan's plan of taking from us our agency.

5. Adversity is a necessity. We shouldn't try to take it away from our family. Life is about making mistakes and learning from them. We must learn from our mistakes and let our loved ones learn from theirs.

6. Sometimes, even when it is not their fault they need to fix it, work it out for themselves. To get through the adversity, to grow from the experience. We deprive them when we fix it for them.

7. We know that the most important responsibility we can have is to raise our children in the way of the Lord. And, again, when they go astray our natural

tendency is to blame ourselves. **Where did we go wrong? we ask. What could we have done differently? None of us are perfect, and we have all made mistakes but, if we have taught them well we have done all we can.**

It may seem contrary to our responsibility when I say we must not help them. But, again, if we have done our job in teaching them as we've raised them, then we have done our job. Now it is up to them to use that agency they have been given by our Heavenly Father, and then be accountable for their actions. Then, the decisions they make are their own, they are not ours.

8. Agency/accountability have not ceased to be a factor in the Lord's eternal plan. Life is about choices and consequences. God's plan of happiness is about choices and consequences.

9. We are living in a society that makes no demands and expects no accountability. In the same family some children choose well and some chose evil. We came to this earth with our agency.

10. We have the power to teach correct principles, but we do not have the power to redeem our children from their poor choices. No matter how much we'd like to, We cannot save people from themselves.

Elder Wolfgang Paul of the Quorum of Seventy sums up it well:

"In order for us to use our agency, we must have a knowledge of good and evil, we must have the freedom to make choices, and after we have exercised our agency, there must be consequences that follow our choices."

Chapter 19 - Onward

Heavenly Father is in charge! He loves us! His plan is one of perfection. His perfect Son gave His life that we might live. The Gospel is true. There is a perfectly laid out Plan of Salvation. And a roadmap to lead us successfully back to their presence when our earthly probation is through.

A tremendous price was paid to allow us to have our agency.

Just as we have our agency to choose our path we must allow our loved ones their agency.

We know from the Lord's relationship with His chosen people that eventually, when they have repented and paid the price for their disobedience the Lord will then open his arms and receive them back.

If we choose our path wisely, we have been given a similar promise.

"The Prophet Joseph Smith declared–and he never taught a more comforting doctrine–that the eternal sealings of faithful parents and the divine promises made to them for valiant service in the Cause of Truth, would save not only themselves, but likewise their posterity. Though some of the sheep may wander, the eye of the Shepherd is upon them, and sooner or later they will feel the tentacles of Divine Providence reaching out after them and drawing them back to the fold. Either in this life or the life to come, they will return. They will have to pay their debt to justice; they will suffer for their sins; and may tread a thorny path; but if it leads them at last, like the penitent Prodigal, to a loving and forgiving father's heart and home, the painful experience will not have been in vain. Pray for your careless and disobedient children; hold on to them with your faith. Hope on, trust on, till you see the salvation of God."
   (Orson F. Whitney, in Conference Report, Apr. 1929, p. 110)

It is my hope that you will carefully consider the messages that are here--that for those with addictions the seemingly contradictory best help is no help. And, that I have helped you understand and cherish the gift of agency. It is my prayer that you allow our Savior to help lighten your heavy heart.

Acknowledgments

Dr. "O" - who taught us, strengthened us, and encouraged us and who finally got us to understand that unconditional love is not what we thought it was.

Washington County Drug Court - Every individual who contributes to the whole of this intensive program that offers hope and a chance when it seems like all hope and chances are gone.

Aaron, and all the counselors at Southwest Center who patiently, and sometimes not so patiently, make us learn the facts, consider the facts, face the facts and dig deep within ourselves. And teach us, that life must–and does--go on.

Family Group Members - who share, vent, cry, and even laugh together.

Cowboy Bob - an amazing equine therapist who lets his "charges" quickly learn that it is impossible to intimidate a thousand pound animal but that you can clearly communicate with it and set boundaries for it. Bob can make a lesson out of anything and everything!!

Addicts - Children of our Heavenly Father. Individuals who are fighting demons the rest of us can't even begin to fathom, but first and foremost, children of our Heavenly Father.

Addicts working on Recovery - Some of the strongest and most determined individuals I have met, and extremely supportive of one another.

Local "Anonymous Groups" whether for alcohol, narcotics, meth, coke, or whatever - and the 12-step groups for their tireless efforts of assisting others in recovery.

"Sponsors" - for being there when you are needed, any hour or any day. The sounding board for your charge in their times of need--stress, despair, and success. Hopefully we all have such a devoted friend to turn to, no matter what our place   in life.

Parents of Addicts - We know there are many, many out there. We know you are hurting. We hope you know, and will truly accept the fact, that what has happened is NOT YOUR FAULT.

Our children - Who all have been kind and loving and caring towards their brother, and supportive of our decisions even when they didn't understand/agree with them. And patient with our efforts and time expenditures in his behalf. Special thanks to his next older brother who has gone to both group meetings and AA meetings in an effort to gain a better understanding of everything.

Our friends - Who have also been supportive and caring, and who continue to extend their friendship to our son, and welcome him when he comes to church.

And finally...
Judge Shumate – there cannot be enough good said about this man, who brought this inspired program to our county.   He has total grasp of the problem and the best possible routes to recovery—the absolute necessity of structure and personal responsibility, as well as a "safety net" as the learning is taking place. He truly cares about those in his charge. He knows them each by name. He has patience when progress, no matter how small, is taking place. He has zero

tolerance for those who continue to try to use (abuse) the program. He is very tough and he is very fair. When the individuals first come into the program they hate him. When they graduate, they are forever indebted to him.

Dave

davengail@infowest.com

2007

Made in the USA
Columbia, SC
20 March 2025